The Countries

Pakistan

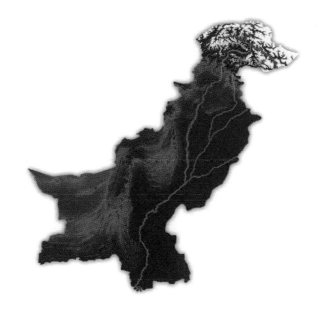

Tamara L. Britton
ABDO Publishing Company

visit us at
www.abdopub.com

Published by ABDO Publishing Company, 4940 Viking Drive, Edina, Minnesota 55435.
Copyright © 2002 by Abdo Consulting Group, Inc. International copyrights reserved in
all countries. No part of this book may be reproduced in any form without written
permission from the publisher.

Printed in the United States.

Photo Credits: Corbis
Art Direction & Maps: Neil Klinepier

Library of Congress Cataloging-in-Publication Data

Britton, Tamara L., 1963-
   Pakistan / Tamara L. Britton.
     p. cm. -- (The countries)
   Includes index.
   Summary: An introduction to the history, geography, government, economy, and
people of Pakistan, a Muslim country in southern Asia. Includes a recipe for barfi, a
dessert.
   ISBN 1-57765-654-7
   1. Pakistan--Juvenile literature. [1. Pakistan.] I. Title. II. Series.

DS376.9 .B74 2002
954.91--dc21

                                             2001055222

Contents

Aadaab!

Hello from Pakistan! Pakistan is a country in southern Asia. Its land contains mountains, **plateaus**, plains, and deserts.

Pakistan's first civilization began in the Indus River valley about 4,000 years ago. In 1757, the British East India Company conquered Pakistan. In 1947, the British divided the land into East Pakistan, West Pakistan, and India. Today, Pakistan is an independent country under military rule.

Pakistan's people are a mix of many different **cultures**. Islam is Pakistan's national religion. Almost all Pakistanis are Muslims. Pakistanis have large, extended families. They enjoy sports, music, and literature. They celebrate many holidays.

Most Pakistanis are farmers. Wheat is Pakistan's major crop. Pakistan's farmers also raise livestock. Pakistanis manufacture goods such as cotton cloth. And they work in service industries.

Pakistan faces many problems. Its **economy** is small. And it owes much money to other nations. But its people are strong, and they are working hard to make Pakistan a great place to work and live.

Aadaab from Pakistan!

Fast Facts

ISLAMABAD

OFFICIAL NAME: The Islamic Republic of Pakistan
CAPITAL: Islamabad

LAND
- Highest Point: Mount Godwin-Austen (K2) 28,251 feet (8,611 m)
- Major River: Indus River
- Desert Regions: Thal, Cholistan, and Thar

PEOPLE
- Population: 144,135,000 (2002 estimate)
- Major Cities: Islamabad, Karachi
- Language: Urdu (Official), Punjabi, English, various regional languages
- Religion: Islam, Christianity, Hinduism

GOVERNMENT
- Form: Federal Republic
- Chief of State: President
- Flag: Green flag with vertical white stripe on the mast side. A large, white crescent and star are in the center of the green field. The crescent and star are symbols of Islam.
- National Anthem: "Qaumi Tarana" ("National Anthem")
- Nationhood: 1947

ECONOMY
- Agricultural Products: Cotton, wheat, rice, sugarcane, fruit, vegetables, meats, dairy products
- Mining Products: Natural gas, petroleum, coal, iron, copper, salt, limestone
- Manufactured Products: Textiles, processed foods, beverages, clothing, paper products
- Money: Rupee (100 paisas = 1 rupee)

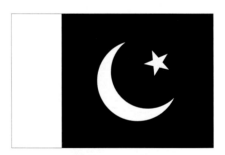

Pakistan's flag

100 Rupee note

Timeline

2000 B.C.	Pakistan's first civilization
327 B.C.	Alexander the Great conquers Pakistan
A.D. 700s	Muslims conquer Pakistan
1757	British conquer Pakistan
1947	British create East Pakistan, West Pakistan, and India
1972	East Pakistan becomes Bangladesh; West Pakistan becomes Pakistan
1977	Mohammad Zia-ul-Haq overthrows government
1988	Benazir Bhutto becomes prime minister and the first woman elected to lead a Muslim nation; Ghulam Ishaq Khan is elected president
1990	Khan accuses Bhutto's government of corruption and removes her from office; Nawaz Sharif becomes prime minister
1993	Khan and Sharif resign their offices; Parliament is dissolved; Bhutto becomes prime minister; Farooq Leghari elected president
1996	Leghari accuses Bhutto's government of corruption and removes Bhutto from office
1997	Sharif becomes prime minister; Mohammad Rafiq Tarar becomes president
1998	Pakistan successfully explodes several nuclear devices
1999	Pakistan and India fight over Kashmir
1999	General Pervez Musharraf leads a military coup, suspends the constitution, and dissolves parliament
2001	Pakistan helps the U.S. in its fight against global terrorism

Pakistan's Past

Pakistan's first civilization began in the Indus River valley about 4,000 years ago. In 327 B.C., Alexander the Great conquered Pakistan. In the A.D. 700s, the first Muslims conquered Pakistan. They ruled Pakistan until the 1700s.

Muhammad Ali Jinnah

In 1757, the British East India Company conquered Pakistan. Under British rule, Pakistan became part of India, a Hindu nation. After World War I, the people began to oppose British rule. In 1940, Muhammad Ali Jinnah led the Muslim League to force the British to create separate Hindu and Muslim nations.

So in 1947, the British divided the land into East Pakistan, West Pakistan, and India. In 1971, East and West Pakistan fought a war. In 1972, East Pakistan became the independent country of Bangladesh. West Pakistan took the name Pakistan.

In 1971, Zulfikar Ali Bhutto ruled Pakistan. But in 1977, Mohammad Zia-ul-Haq led a **coup**. He ruled Pakistan until he died in 1988.

Zulfikar Ali Bhutto

Benazir Bhutto

That year, Benazir Bhutto, Zulfikar Ali Bhutto's daughter, became **prime minister**. She was the first woman elected to lead a Muslim nation. But she was forced out in 1990. Nawaz Sharif became prime minister.

In July 1993, Sharif resigned. The people elected a new **parliament** in October. Bhutto's Pakistan People's Party won the most seats, and she became prime minister again. In November, Farooq Leghari was elected president.

But in November 1996, Leghari accused Bhutto's government of **corruption**. He removed her from office. In 1997, Sharif again became prime minister. Later that year, Mohammad Rafiq Tarar became president.

In May 1998, India successfully carried out several **nuclear** tests. Pakistan responded by exploding several nuclear devices of its own.

Nawaz Sharif

A year later, fighting broke out between Pakistani and Indian troops in the Kashmir region. Both Pakistan and India claimed the territory. In July 1999, Sharif withdrew Pakistan's army from the area. But India and Pakistan continued to argue over possession of the region.

That same year, Sharif fired General Pervez Musharraf, who was army chief of staff. He then tried to prevent an airplane carrying Musharraf from landing in Pakistan.

In October 1999, Musharraf led a military **coup**, which overthrew the government. Musharraf said he carried out the coup to stop government **corruption**. He broke up the **parliament** and suspended the **constitution**. Then he declared himself the head of the government.

On September 11, 2001, terrorists associated with Osama bin Laden's al-Qaeda terrorist organization attacked the United States. Bin Laden and al-Qaeda were based in Afghanistan, Pakistan's northern neighbor. The U.S. wanted to attack al-Qaeda in Afghanistan, but needed Musharraf's help.

Musharraf agreed to allow U.S. military aircraft to fly through Pakistani airspace. He also allowed the United States to establish air bases in Pakistan. In return, the U.S. lifted the **economic sanctions** it had imposed when Pakistan tested its **nuclear** devices.

Pervez Musharraf

The Land

Pakistan is in southern Asia. Iran borders Pakistan on the southwest. Afghanistan lies to Pakistan's west and north. China is on Pakistan's northeast, and India lies to the east. On Pakistan's southern border lies the Arabian Sea.

Pakistan's land contains mountains, **plateaus**, plains, and deserts. In the north are the Himalaya mountains. From these mountains, the land slopes down to a plain. This plain is the largest agricultural region in Pakistan. It runs south along the Indus River to the Arabian Sea.

A glacier in the Himalaya

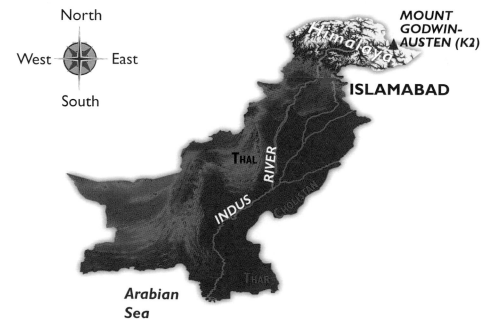

Deserts extend from the plains to the Arabian Sea. The three desert regions are the Thal, the Cholistan, and the Thar.

Pakistan's largest river is the Indus. It flows south from Tibet through Pakistan to the Arabian Sea. The Indus River divides Pakistan into eastern and western halves.

Pakistan has a continental climate. This means it has hot summers and cold winters. However, Pakistan's climate is affected by the land's different elevations. In the mountains, the summers are cool and the winters are very cold. In the deserts, the summers are very hot and the winters are cool.

The Thal Desert

Rain

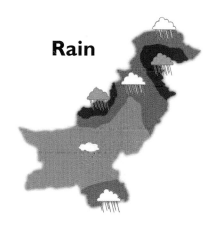

Rainfall

AVERAGE YEARLY RAINFALL

Inches		*Centimeters*
Under 10		Under 25
10 - 20		25 - 50
20 - 59		50 - 150

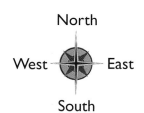

North

West   East

South

Temperature

AVERAGE TEMPERATURE

Summer

Fahrenheit		*Celsius*
over 68°		over 20°
50° - 68°		10° - 20°
32° - 50°		0° - 10°
14° - 32°		-10° - 0°

Winter

Wild Things

Pakistan's varied land is home to many plants and animals. In the mountainous north, **coniferous** forests cover the land. Brown and black bears live

there, including the Himalayan black bear. Leopards, Siberian ibex, and many kinds of sheep also live in the mountains.

In the south, dry grasses and scrub trees grow. Some forested areas lie along the Indus River. The Indus River dolphin lives in this river. This type of dolphin is six to eight feet (2 to 2.5 m) long and weighs about 200 pounds (90 kg).

A Siberian ibex

The Indus River dolphin is blind. It finds its way through the water using **echolocation**. It searches the river's bottom, looking for food. It eats **prawns**, carp, catfish, and small **crustaceans**.

Dams along the Indus River divided the dolphins into small groups and increased water pollution. The dams have caused a sharp decline in the dolphin population. But the Indus River Dolphin Reserve in the Sind Province provides a safe place for the dolphins to live and grow.

A Himalayan black bear

Pakistan's People

Pakistan was once a part of India. The British government divided India into three separate countries. So today, Pakistan's people are a mix of many different **cultures**.

A Pakistani family

Islam is Pakistan's national religion. Almost all Pakistanis are Muslim. But there are non-Muslim Pakistanis, including Christians and Hindus.

The Kalasha are a non-Muslim tribe. They live in the Kalash Valley. These people live in houses made of wood, stone, and mud. They grow grains and raise goats.

In Pakistan, most families consist of a father, mother, their unmarried children, and their married sons and their families. These families all live together in the same house. The men are in charge of the household. They make all the important decisions. Women take care of the families. They clean the house, wash the clothes, and prepare the meals.

Pakistanis enjoy a varied diet based on grains. They eat baked and fried breads. Lentils and other **legumes** are popular, too. *Dhal* is a type of stew made with lentils. *Samosas* are dough pockets stuffed with beef, mutton, or chicken. The most common dessert is *barfi*.

Pakistan has no education laws. Children do not have to attend school. Primary education is free. But less than half of Pakistan's children go to school. Because of their lack of education, many Pakistanis are **illiterate**.

A Kalasha woman cooks bread in her home

Barfi

1 cup ground almonds
1 cup ground cashews
1 cup sugar
1 can evaporated milk
1/4 cup butter

Melt the butter in a heavy skillet on medium heat. Stir in the milk and bring to a boil, stirring constantly. Turn heat to low and cook until milk thickens. Add nuts and sugar. Cook for 10 minutes, stirring constantly. Pour *barfi* onto a flat, buttered dish. When cool, cut into diamond shapes.

AN IMPORTANT NOTE TO THE CHEF: Always have an adult help with the preparation and cooking of food. Never use kitchen utensils or appliances without adult permission and supervision.

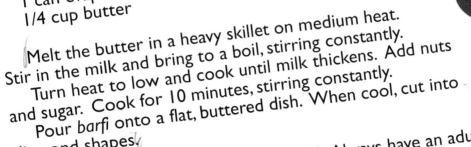

English	Urdu
Hello	Aadaab
Goodbye	Khuda hafiz
Yes	Achchha
No	La
Thank you	Mehrbaani
Please	Khush karna
Mother	Maan
Father	Baaba

LANGUAGE

Making Money

Pakistan's **economy** is based on agriculture, manufacturing, and services. Only a small part of Pakistan's land is fit to grow crops. But more than half of all Pakistanis work in agriculture. Pakistanis grow wheat, sugarcane, rice, and cotton. They also raise goats, sheep, cattle, and poultry. Pakistan has the world's largest canal **irrigation** system.

Pakistanis manufacture **textiles**. Textiles are Pakistan's chief manufactured product and leading export. They also manufacture sugar, tires, cement, bicycles, and **ghee**.

Service industries employ less than half of all Pakistanis. These industries are especially important in the large cities. Service industries include education, finance, government, health care, and transportation.

Harvesting wheat in Pakistan

Cities

Karachi is Pakistan's largest city and main port. Karachi is located on the coast of the Arabian Sea. About six million people live there.

Most of Karachi's people work in manufacturing and trade. They make clothes, shoes, machinery, leather and rubber products, and processed foods. They also build cars and ships.

Almost all of Pakistan's sea trade leaves from Karachi's port. The port also handles the sea trade of Pakistan's neighbor, Afghanistan. There are many markets in Karachi's center. There, people sell carpets, clothing, leather products, and crafts.

When they are not working, Karachi's people enjoy many leisure activities. The Pakistan Arts Council is located in Karachi. The zoological gardens and National Museum also draw many visitors. The

View over central Karachi

University of Karachi's library is one of Pakistan's largest libraries. There are many beach resorts along Karachi's coast. The dome of the Defence Housing Society **Mosque** is one of the largest in the world.

Islamabad is Pakistan's capital. About 500,000 people live there. Islamabad is the center of Pakistan's government. The Presidential Palace, National **Assembly** building, and Supreme Court buildings draw many visitors. Pakistan's Atomic Research Institute is in Islamabad. So is the National Health Center.

Lahore is Pakistan's **cultural**, educational, and artistic center. It has parks and gardens, crowded streets, and **bazaars**. It is also home to the Lahore Museum, Pakistan's best and biggest museum.

Horse-drawn carriages make their way through a crowded street in Lahore, Pakistan.

Pakistan on the Go

Pakistan has 5,073 miles (8,163 km) of railway. Many Pakistanis travel by train. But the trains do not go into the mountains. So Pakistanis must use other types of transportation in these areas.

Pakistan has 154,015 miles (247,811 km) of highways. But few Pakistanis have private cars. So most people travel by bus, taxi, **rickshaw**, or *tonga*. *Tongas* are two-wheeled carts pulled by horses.

Pakistan's government controls the airlines. Pakistan International Airlines (PIA) has about 50 aircraft. The planes travel to other countries and many Pakistani cities.

Driver with his auto-rickshaw

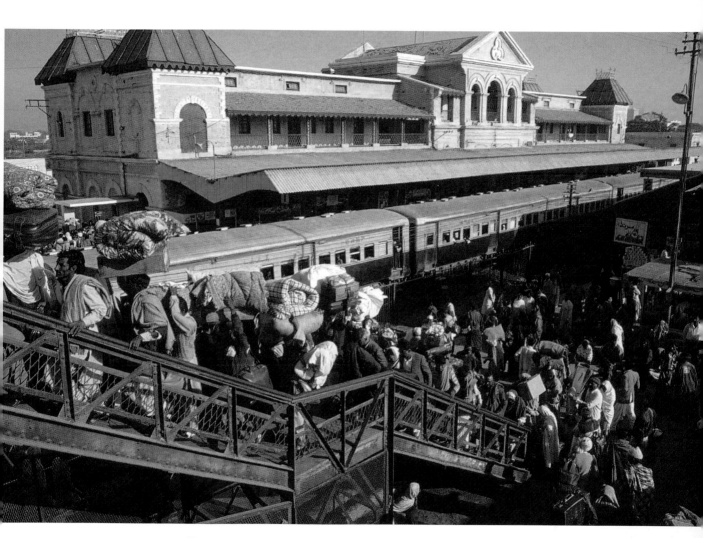

*Travelers slowly make their way up a stairway
at the busy Karachi railway station.*

Pakistan's Government

Before the military took over Pakistan's government in 1999, Pakistan had a **democratically** elected government. It was ruled by the **constitution** of 1973.

In the **executive** branch, a **prime minister** headed the country's government. A president served as head of state. The prime minister appointed a **cabinet** to help run the government.

The **legislative** branch of the government consisted of a two-house **parliament**. The Senate had 87 members. They were elected by provincial **assemblies**. The National Assembly had 217 members. They were elected by general vote. Pakistanis over age 25 were allowed to vote.

Pakistan's **judicial** system was made up of **civil**, criminal, and appeals courts. The Supreme Court was the nation's highest court.

Today, Pakistan is still under military rule. Its **parliament** does not meet, and its **constitution** is still suspended.

The government complex in Islamabad

Let's Celebrate!

Since Pakistan is an Islamic **republic**, most of its holidays are Islamic celebrations. Because Islam follows a lunar calendar, the dates of these holidays are different each year. Most Pakistanis observe Ramadan. During Ramadan, Muslims do not eat, drink, or smoke between sunrise and sunset.

The beginning of Eid al-Fitr ends the great fast of Ramadan. During this holiday, Muslims feast and show goodwill to the poor.

Eid al-Azha celebrates Abraham's willingness to sacrifice his son Isaac to please **Allah**. On this day, each family sacrifices an animal. They divide the meat into three parts. The family, their relatives, and the poor each receive a part.

Opposite page: Faithful Pakistani Muslims pray outside a mosque in Karachi during the first day of Eid al-Fitr.

Pakistani Culture

Pakistan's **culture** offers its people many ways to relax. Cricket is Pakistan's national sport. Cricket is a baseball-like game played with bats, balls, and wickets. Two teams of 11 players each take turns hitting a hard, leather ball. Each game consists of two innings and may last several days.

Children practice cricket pitching and batting skills. They would like to be champions, like Pakistan's Hanif Mohammad and Imran Khan. Mohammad holds the world's record for the most points scored in a cricket game.

Children also like to fly kites. They fashion kites from paper, cloth, and sticks or twigs. Their skillful construction methods ensure that kites made from scavenged materials can fly.

Pakistanis also relax by watching television. Most homes in Pakistan have at least one television. In big cities, Pakistanis enjoy going to the movies.

Pakistani players compete in a cricket tournament.

Glossary

Allah - the Islamic word for God.
assembly - a company of persons gathered for discussion and legislation.
bazaar - a place for the sale of goods.
cabinet - a group of advisers chosen by the president, prime minister, or head of state to lead government departments.
civil - of or relating to the state or its citizens.
conifer - a tree or shrub that has cones. Pine, spruce, hemlock, and larch are conifers.
constitution - the laws that govern a nation.
corrupt - to be influenced by other people to be dishonest.
coup - a sudden, successful military act that overthrows a government.
crustacean - any group of animals with hard shells that live mostly in water. Crabs, lobsters, and shrimp are crustaceans.
culture - the customs, arts, and tools of a nation or people at a certain time.
democracy - a governmental system in which the people vote on how to run the country.
echolocation - a process for locating distant or unseen objects by means of sound waves.
economy - the way a colony, city, state, or nation uses its money, goods, and natural resources.
executive - the branch of a government that puts laws into effect.
ghee - a purified butter.
illiterate - having little or no education and unable to read or write.
irrigate - to supply land with water by using channels, streams, and pipes.
judicial - the branch of a government that administers the laws.
legislative - the branch of a government that makes the laws.
legume - the fruit or seed of plants such as peas or beans used for food.
mosque - a Muslim place of worship.

nuclear - of or relating to atomic energy.
parliament - the highest lawmaking body of some governments.
plateau - a raised area of flat land.
prawn - a large shrimp.
prime minister - the highest-ranked member of some governments.
republic - a form of government in which authority rests with voting citizens and is carried out by elected officials such as a parliament.
rickshaw - a small, covered, two-wheeled vehicle usually for one passenger and is pulled by one person.
sanction - a measure taken against a nation that has disobeyed international law. Sanctions are meant to force the offending nation to obey the law.
textile - of or having to do with the designing, manufacturing, or producing of woven fabric.

Web Sites

Government of Pakistan's official site.
http://www.pak.gov.pk/public/country_profile.html
Learn about Pakistan's history, people, and culture at the official site of the Pakistani government.

Pakistan Tourism Development Corporation
http://www.tourism.gov.pk/
Tourist information from the Pakistani government.

These sites are subject to change. Go to your favorite search engine and type in Pakistan for more sites.

Index